UP CLOSE

BUGS & BUTTERFLIES

A CLOSE-UP PHOTOGRAPHIC LOOK INSIDE YOUR WORLD

Quarto is the authority on a wide range of topics.
Quarto educates, entertains and enriches the lives of our readers—enthusiasts and lovers of hands-on living.
www.quartoknows.com

Published by Walter Foster Jr., an imprint of Quarto Publishing Group USA Inc.

Project Editor: Heidi Fiedler
Written by Heidi Fiedler

Cover photography by Dušan Beno.
Photographs on pages 8, 10, 14, 16, 32–34, 46, 49, 54, and 60 by Dušan Beno.
Photograph on page 38 by Miron Karlinsky.
Photographs on pages 18, 24, 36, 40, 42, 50–51, 52, 56 by Igor Siwanowicz.
All other images © Shutterstock.

6 Orchard Road, Suite 100
Lake Forest, CA 92630
quartoknows.com
Visit our blogs @quartoknows.com

Printed in China
3 5 7 9 10 8 6 4 2

Are You Ready for Your Close-up?

Can you feel your brain tickling? That's the magic of looking at something way UP CLOSE. It transforms the ordinary into something new and strange, and inspires everyone from hi-tech shutterbugs and supersmart scientists to look again. So let's turn the ZOOM up to eleven and discover a whole new way of seeing the world.

How Eye See the World

"Whatcha lookin' at?" That's the question people have been asking each other for thousands of years. The first humans observed interesting—and important—things like woolly mammoths, lightning, and each other. Early artists moved on to painting and drawing what they saw. Finally, in 1862, photography allowed people to capture what they saw in new and amazing ways.

Today, photographs are everywhere. Cereal boxes, bulletin boards, and T-shirts are all home to photos. A simple image search online can produce cootchie-cootchie-coo images of bright-eyed babies or stark, white, snowy landscapes. Photographers capture everything from moments of joy and pain to the wonders that exist in the cracks and hidden layers of our busy world. They focus their attention on a huge range of subjects, and the images they produce reveal how everyone sees the world in their own unique way.

The History of Photography

Black-and-White Photography

1839
Daguerreotypes capture rough images.

1859
Photography goes panoramic.

1862
Nicéphore Niépce creates the first photograph. It takes 8 hours.

1877
Eadweard Muybridge invents a way to shoot objects—such as horses—in motion.

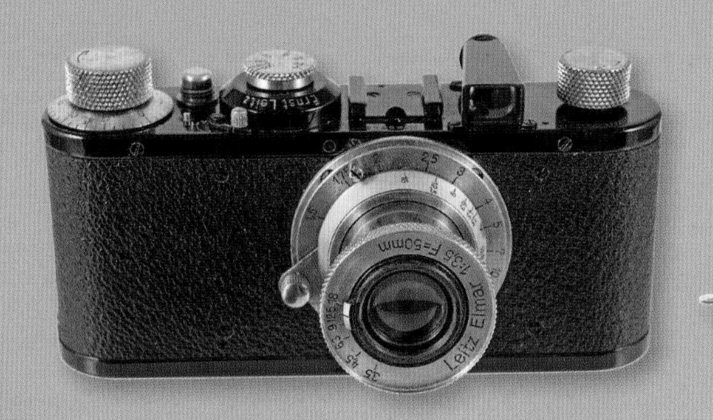

Color Photography

1888
Kodak™ produces the first mass-produced camera.

1912
The 35mm camera takes center stage.

1930
Flash bulbs help photographers capture images in low light.

1935
New techniques make color photography shine.

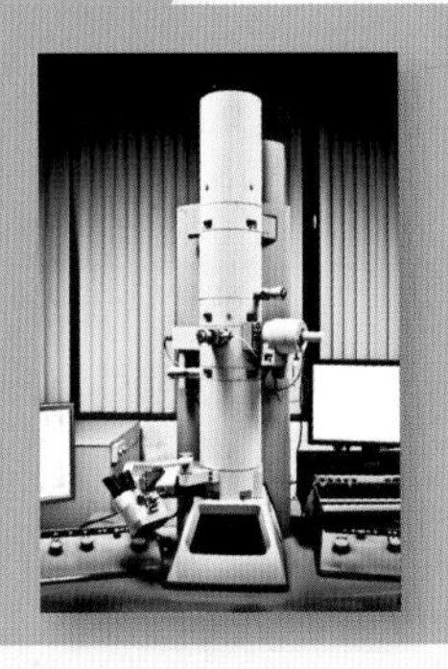

1939
An electron microscope reveals what a virus looks like.

1946
Zoomar produces the zoom lens.

Digital Photography

1976
Canon® produces the first camera with a microprocessor.

"Photography...has little to do with the things you see and everything to do with the way you see them."
–Elliott Erwitt

1992
The first JPEG is produced.

2015
Instagram is home to more than 20 billion images.

Extreme Close-up!

Photography has been helping people express how they see the world for nearly 200 years, and in that time, things have gone way beyond taking a simple shot of a horse or a sunset. Today, photographers are pushing the limits of technology.

Macro photographers use large lenses to get WAY up close to their subjects. They can magnify an object to more than five times its size, using special lenses that reveal patterns and textures that wow viewers.

Micro photography goes even further. It uses a microscope to reveal details humans could never see before. It can make a beetle look like a glowing planet or a priceless piece of jewelry.

With their vibrant colors and strange shapes, bugs and butterflies are a favorite subject for photographers. Some shutterbugs are scientists who are thrilled to be able to count exactly how many lenses are in a compound eye. Other photographers are insect enthusiasts who are obsessed with capturing every hair on a spider. Together, their images help us see the natural world in a whole new way.

Getting the Shot

Photographers choose where and how they want to work based on what type of images they want to produce.

Out in the Field

Macro photographers can take their giant lenses outside to capture insects in their natural environment.

In the Studio

Working inside lets photographers have more control over the lighting, the angle of the camera, and their subject.

Under the Microscope

A microscope allows photographers to look at their subjects in even more detail.

Only the bravest of warriors dare to walk through.
For the legends warn of
Crunching!
Crushing!
And...chomping?

Behold The Hornet

Kill. Chew. Spit. That's how hornets feed their young. Workers take down flies, bees, and other insects. Then they chew them up and feed them to the younger hornets. The hornet's sharp mouth is perfectly shaped for snapping up prey. A single pinch can rip the head off an insect that stands in its way. Working together, they're a force to be reckoned with. A team of 30 Japanese hornets has been known to destroy a colony of 30,000 bees in a few hours.

Electric Colors

Photographers love hornets' bright colors. But these colors aren't just spectacular to look at, they're positively electric! Brown patches absorb sunlight. Yellow areas turn the sunlight into electricity. Scientists are studying the process to learn how it works.

Scientific Name: Vespa
Size: 1.25 inches
Habitat: Paper-like nests they build everywhere except the coldest places
Diet: Tree sap, insects

Hornets' natural **speed** and **strength** inspired **scientists** to make a sports **drink** for human **athletes.**

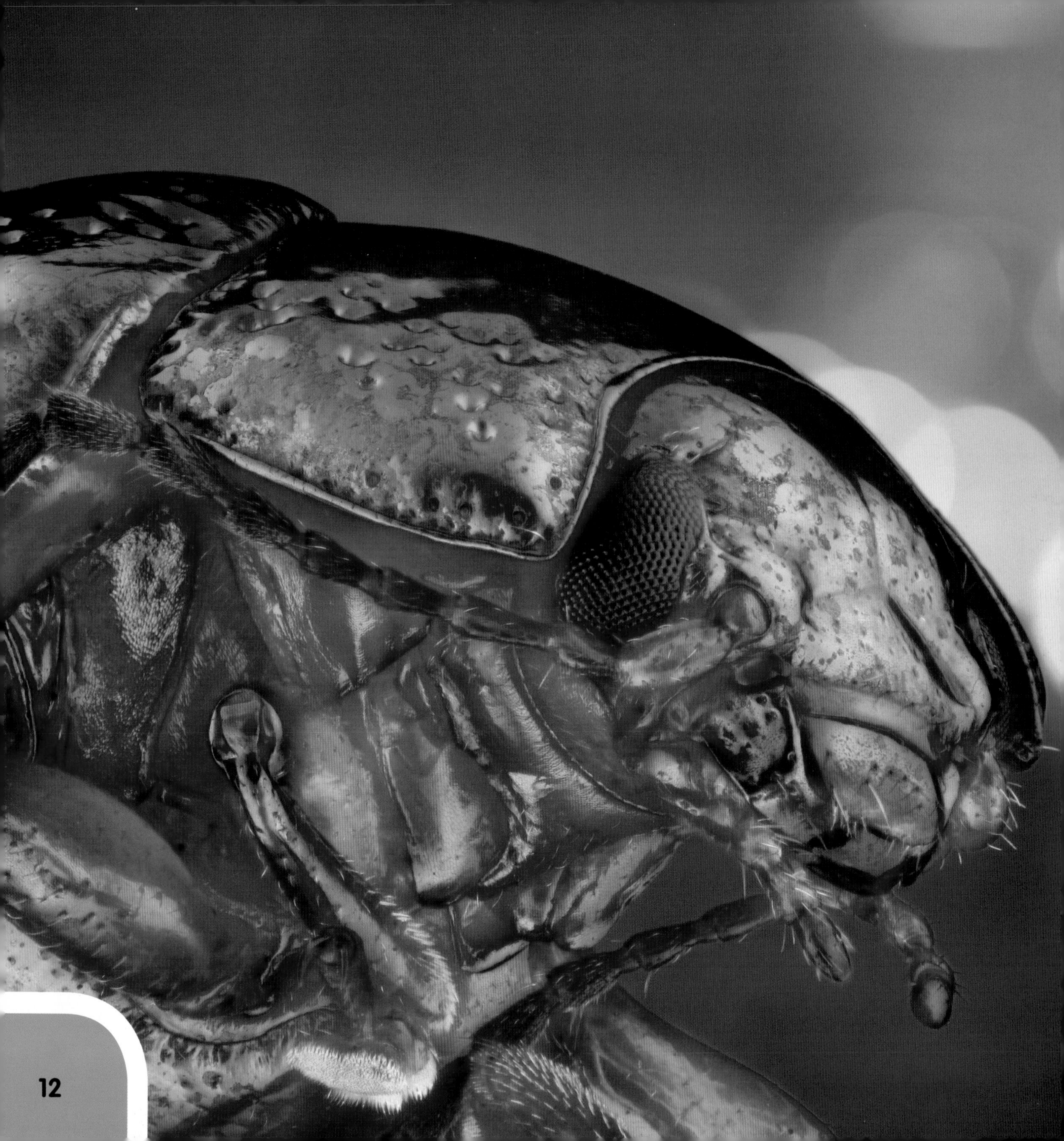

Get a Whiff of That!

Beetles are mind-bogglingly common. Nearly a fifth of all plants and animals are beetles! Rosemary beetles are just one kind. They don't smell like rosemary—they eat it. (Much to the annoyance of gardeners everywhere.) But not everyone is trying to shoo these beauties away. For hundreds of years, brave fashionistas have worn beetles on their shoulders as a unique form of living jewelry.

Beetles may look pretty, but they have developed some major defenses. The bombardier beetle sprays acid from its butt!

Scientific Name: Chrysolina americana
Size: .2 to .3 inches
Habitat: Most land and freshwater areas
Diet: Rosemary and other plants

Buzz Off!

When bark beetles began destroying forests in Canada, scientists struck back. They recorded the sound the beetles made when fighting and played it back at them. The nasty sound scared them away.

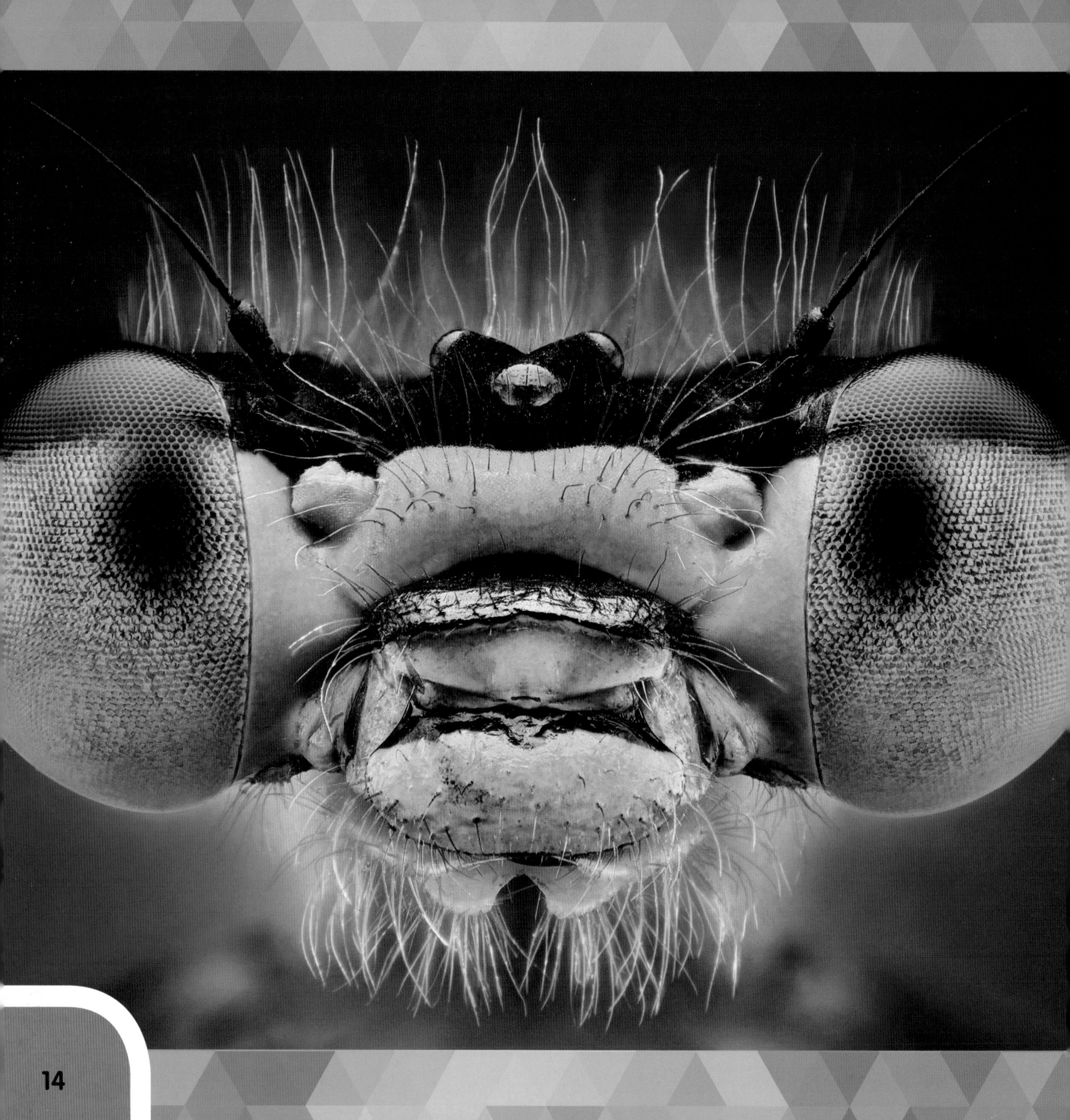

The Blue Dragon

The southern hawker is the largest dragonfly in the world. It's an expert flyer, spiraling through the air to catch prey in flight. It can even fly backward. What can't this blue beast do? So far, no one has seen it breathe fire—at least not yet.

Scientific Name: Aeshna cyanea
Size: 2.75 inches
Habitat: Ponds, lakes, and woodlands in Western Europe
Diet: Insects, tadpoles, and small fish

Some entomologists spend so much time with bugs that they can tell them apart just by smelling them!

Creepycrawology

Southern hawkers are famous for being curious about people. What do bugs call insects that study humans? We may never know. But we do know scientists that study insects are called entomologists.

Gulp!

It's called a black fly, but in the right light, its iridescent body is shockingly green. This particular fly has found the perfect spot to stop for a juicy bite of lunch.

Scientific Name: Simuliidae
Size: .2 to .3 inches
Habitat: Everywhere from Australia to the Arctic
Diet: Blood, nectar, and other plant sugars

Most flies take to the sky in the days between Mother's Day and Father's Day, when it gets warm.

Oooh...Shiny!

When some insects move, they seem to change color and look more like shimmering jewels than creepy critters. Their bodies are iridescent. When light hits the thin, tiny layers that make up their exoskeletons, it's reflected at all different angles, making these areas shine like metal. Other layers separate the light into colorful rainbows. The effect? Common house flies that shine as bright as diamonds.

Wings Up!

The tussock caterpillar is a triple threat. Its wide antennae intimidate predators. A toxic chemical on the body stings anyone who dares to touch it. And this red-headed beast isn't afraid to bite anyone in its path.

Giddy Up!

Scientists used a treadmill and an X-ray machine to figure out how caterpillars move without bones, muscles, or legs. They found the organs inside caterpillars slide forward. Then the outside of the body swings forward.

Scientific Name: Orgyia leucostigma
Size: 1 to 1.5 inches
Habitat: Canada and the United States
Diet: Tree leaves, shrubs, vines, and grasses

Caterpillars scare **predators** by **clicking**, **squeaking**, and **whistling** as they **work** their way **across** their leafy **territory**.

Must. Eat. Dead. Plants.

The millipede may look like a million-legged monster. And it makes its home in piles of dead leaves and feeds on dead plants. But millipedes are actually life-savers. Their digestion process breaks down rotting material into tiny pieces. Then the decomposed bits they leave behind help make the soil healthy for the next generation of plants to grow.

Scientific Name: Diplopoda
Size: 1 to 14 inches
Habitat: Moist areas in chaparral, forests, and grasslands around the world
Diet: Dead leaves and rotting wood

Millipedes curl into a tight ball to avoid predators.

Red Means Stop

Most millipedes are brown or black, but the most poisonous ones are brightly colored.

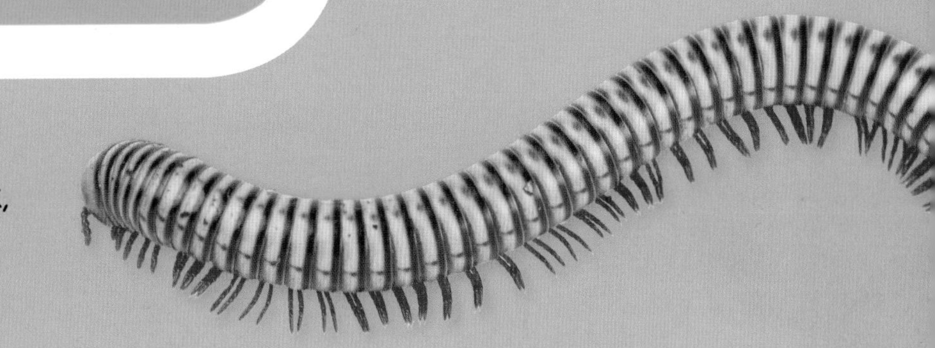

A Golden Time Machine

Every caterpillar is preparing for the day when it will enter its cocoon, turn into a butterfly, and fly away. As a caterpillar grows, it sheds its skin. When the time is right, it shakes off its skin one last time, and a cocoon is revealed. At first it's soft and wet, but soon it hardens. What happens inside is a mystery that scientists are only just beginning to understand.

Cocoons, or **chrysalises**, may look **sleepy**, but if you **watch** carefully, you may **see** them **wiggle** as they **hang** down from the branches.

Cocoons

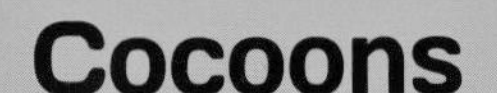

Cocoons come in as many shapes and sizes as butterflies do. Some look like jellybeans. Others look like snail shells or gold pieces of pasta. And many cocoons change colors as the butterfly grows inside.

Sleeping Beauty

When it's time for a butterfly to leave its cocoon, it pushes its head and legs through the wall. Finally, its wings emerge. At first, they look wet and wrinkled. But as the butterfly pumps blood into the veins, the wings expand to reveal their beautiful colors.

Wigging Out

Sure, the butterfly or moth that emerges from a cocoon can be a dull brown insect. But if you're a giant peacock moth, that won't do. You'll want your antennae to look like the leaves from a tree on a distant planet. Big sunglass-style eyes are totally in. And as for your head? Ooh, la, la. The fluffier the better.

Scientific Name: Saturnia pyri
Size: Wingspan is 4 to 6 inches
Habitat: Europe
Diet: Adults don't feed

Polyphemus moths use their long antennae to find a mate and sense chemicals in the air.

Wild Wings

It's hard to look at a caterpillar and know what kind of moth is going to pop out of the cocoon. The bright green caterpillar might turn into an orange moth, a red moth, or one of the other beauties below.

Reporting for Duty

This warrior's eyelashes may be long, but his horns are longer. And he's not afraid to use them. The rain beetle is a fierce member of the beetle family. It lives in colonies that work together as well as any army in the world. Just like all beetles, they are admired for their strength. Some can lift objects hundreds of times heavier than their own weight. Research suggests the bigger the horns, the stronger the beetle.

Scientific Name: Pleocoma puncticollis
Size: 1 to 1.5 inches
Habitat: Western North America
Diet: Adults don't feed

Adult beetles have been known to eat their young if they cry for food too often.

Hear Me Roar!

Crickets, grasshoppers, and cicadas are famous for their chirps. But when it comes to making music, the horned passalus beetle rules. They rub their wings against their abdomen to communicate and hiss when threatened. Scientists have counted them making 17 distinct sounds—more than any other insect.

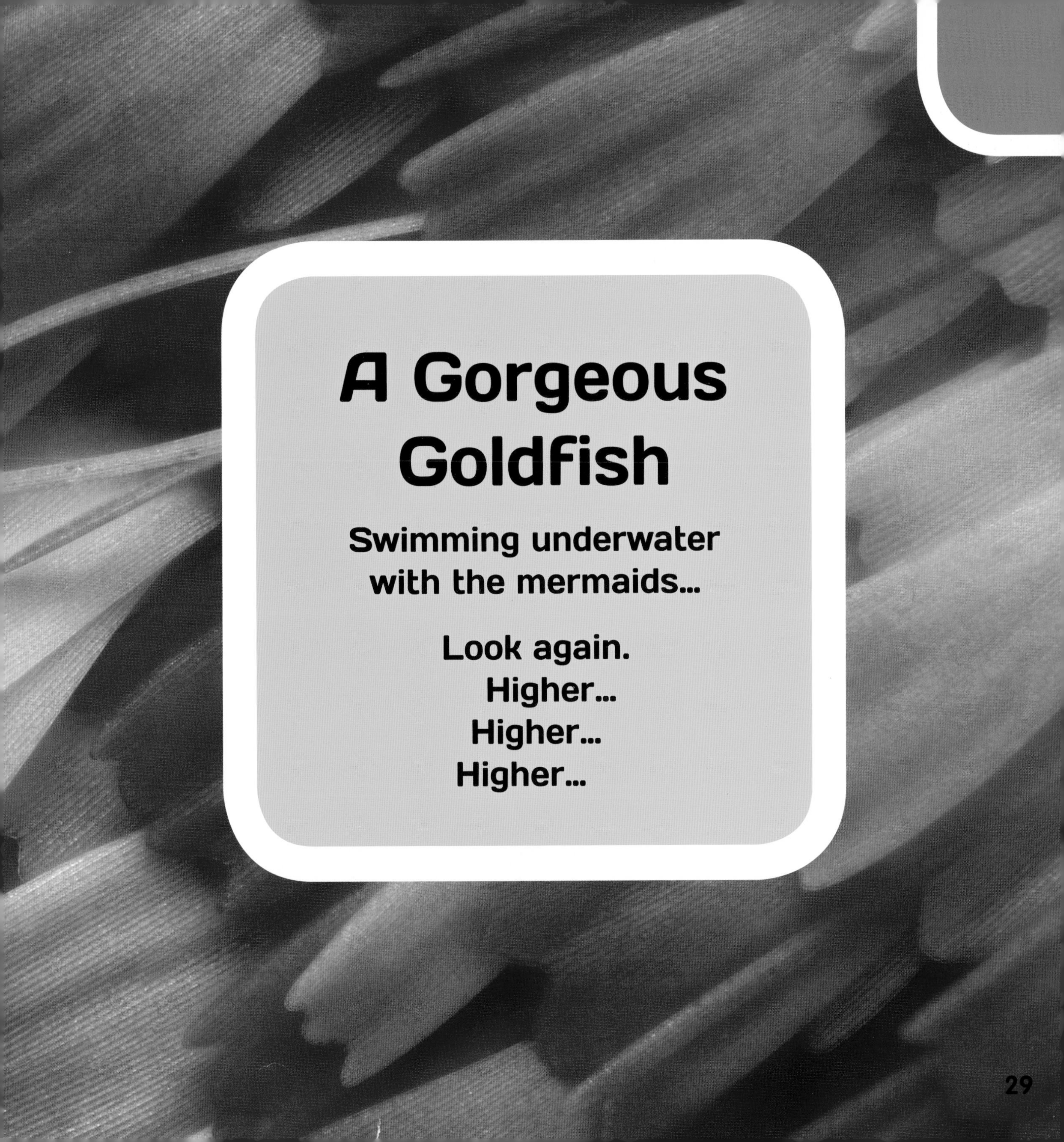

A Gorgeous Goldfish

Swimming underwater
with the mermaids...

Look again.
Higher...
Higher...
Higher...

It's a Rainbow in the Sky!

Butterflies are the fashionistas of the insect world, showing off their couture colors as they fly through the air. But their bright wings aren't just for show. They help butterflies attract mates, scare away predators, and hide among the flowers.

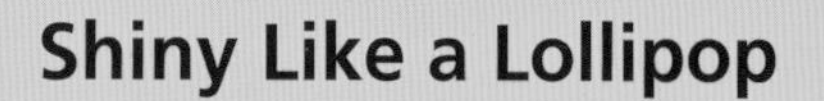

Shiny Like a Lollipop

Mint Chocolate Glamour

The Stunning Swallowtail

A Magnificent Monarch

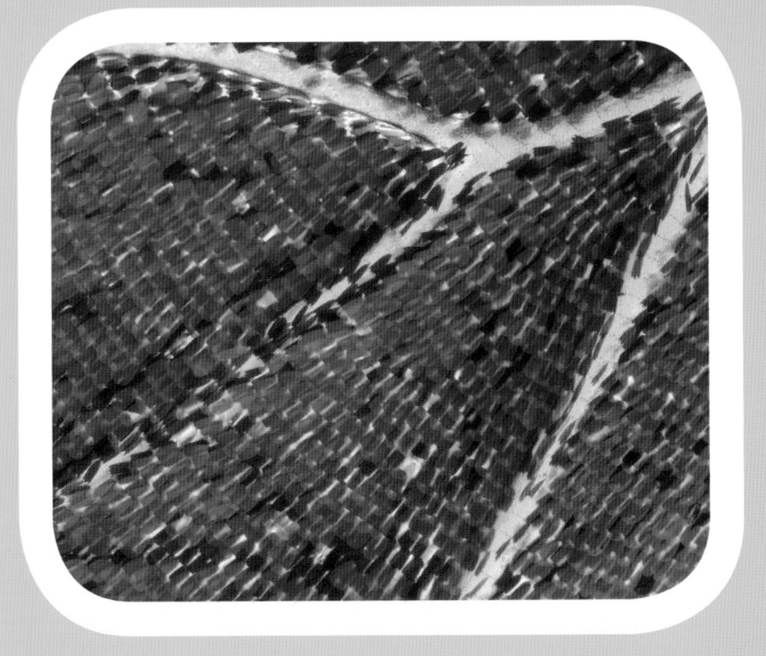

Royal Bloodlines

Fairy Wings

I See You.

What Are You Looking At?

Haven't you ever seen a spider with eight eyes before? In addition to the four eyes on the front of their head, jumping spiders have four more, smaller eyes on top of their heads. This gives them excellent vision, which makes it all the better to see you with, my dear.

Scientific Name: Salticidae
Size: .5 to 1 inch
Habitat: Found around the world
Diet: A variety of small insects

You say "Jump!" and this spider says "How high?" Jumping spiders can jump 50 times their body length. That would be like you jumping across a basketball court!

Webs? Who Needs Them!

Unlike most spiders, jumping spiders don't spin webs. Instead, they use their silk to build a tent to sleep in or survive bad weather. Females build a silk sac to keep their eggs safe.

Say "Cheese!"

Jumping spiders are poised to pounce, which can make it difficult for scientists to study them. That's where photographers come in.

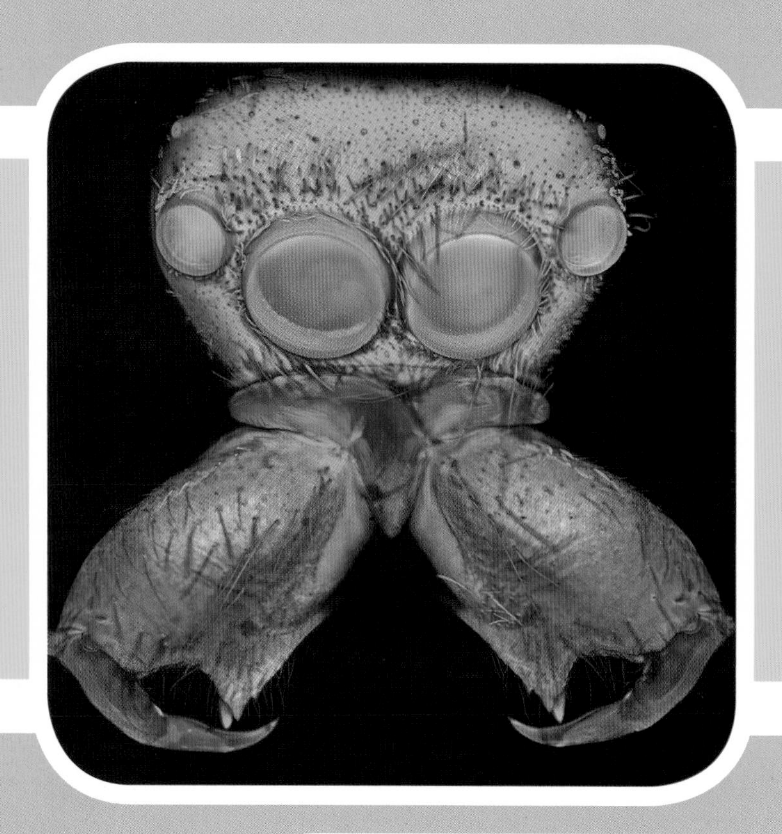

Inside

Scientists use lasers and dyes to study what lies below the furry surface of a spider. In this image, the different colors in the legs and head reflect the various types of chitin, a hard substance that is found in a spider's exoskeleton. The bright red and orange spots are the eyes. They're reflecting the light coming from the microsope.

Outside

Male jumping spiders often have bright streaks of color on their head, jaw, and legs. These colors help them attract a mate.

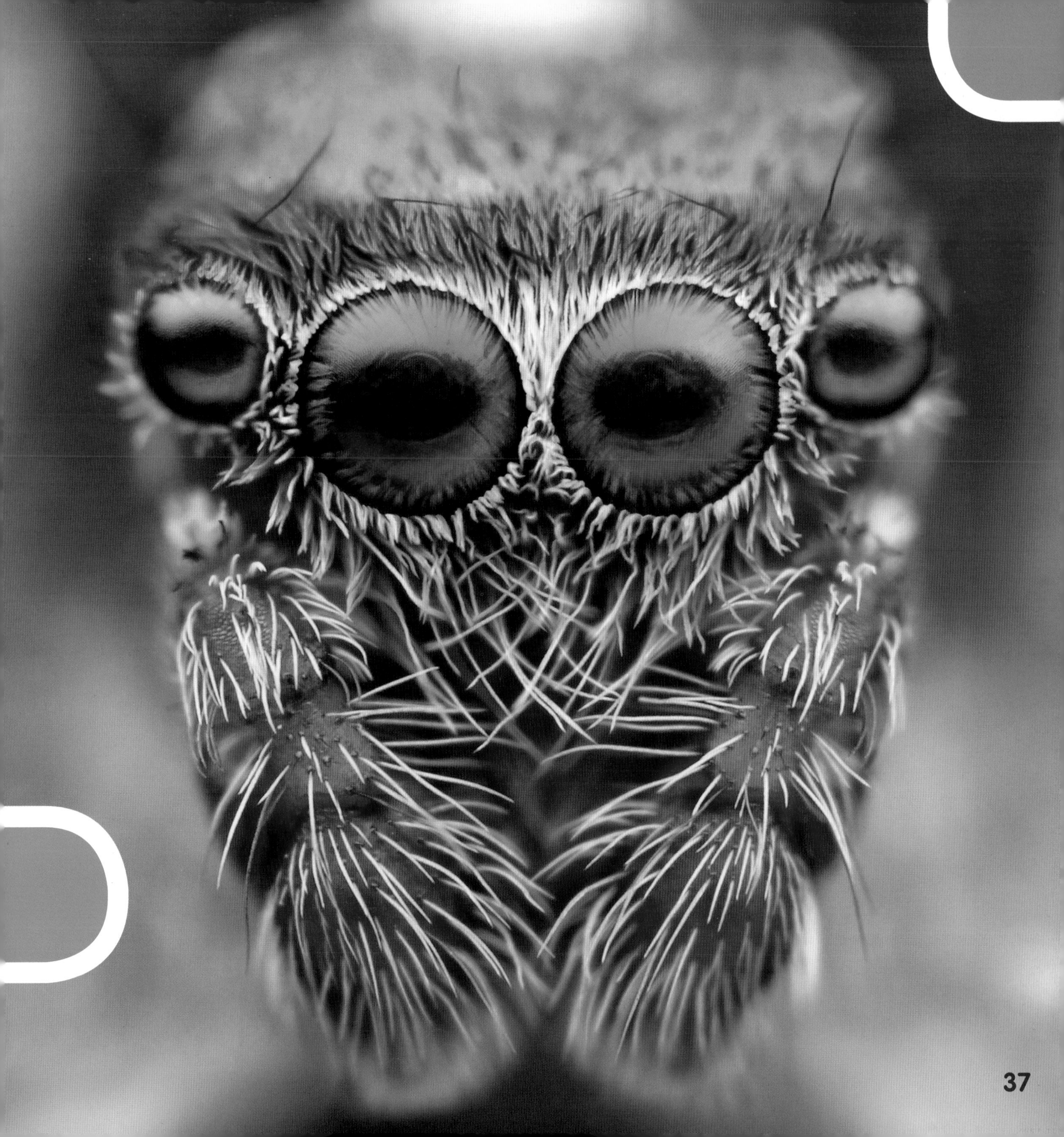

Liftoff!

Like a helicopter poised to take to the sky, this insect is ready for flight. The thorax of these fighter pilots is packed with muscles that enable them to change direction in a hundredth of a second. With just two wings, this thick-headed fly can hover, rotate in place, fly backwards, and upside-down!

Babies that Bite

When it's time for thick-headed flies to raise their young, females find another insect to act as a host. But this isn't a happy party. The female flies jam their eggs into the host's abdomen. When the eggs hatch, the larvae eat their host from the inside out.

Scientific Name: Conopidae
Size: .2 to 1 inch
Habitat: Great Britain and Ireland
Diet: Adults drink flower nectar

Engineers and **scientists** are **working** together to **develop** winged **robots** that can **fly** as well as **insects**.

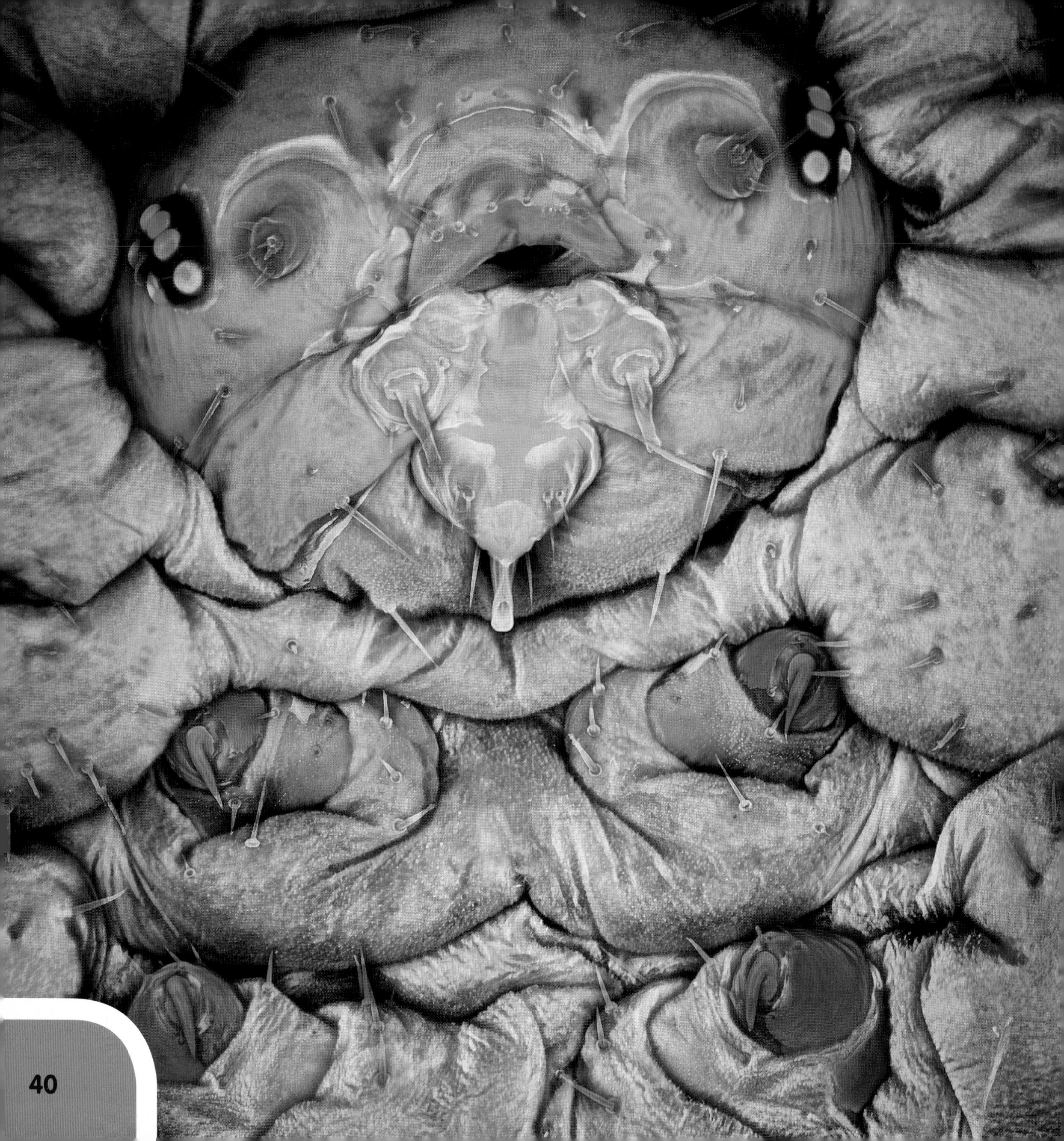

Stuck Between a Camera and a Hard Place

Unlike most caterpillars, which have way too many legs to count, the slug-moth caterpillar has stubby feet that act like suction cups as it travels. They let the caterpillar ripple across leaves at surprisingly high speeds and hang from the underside of the plants it's devouring. Stinging bristles on its back warn anyone who might dare interfere with its meal to stand down.

Yum or Yuck?

Can you guess which of these buggy bites people like eating?

A) ant popcorn
B) beetle sandwiches
C) cricket tacos
D) banana worm bread
E) all of the above

If you answered E, all of the above, you're right!

Scientific Name: Limacodidae
Size: .39 to 1.18 inches
Habitat: Found around the world, especially in the tropics
Diet: The leaves of a variety of plants

In natural light, this caterpillar looks like a chubby, neon green leaf. When it becomes a butterfly, the slug moth is covered in fuzzy, lucky-clover-green streaks.

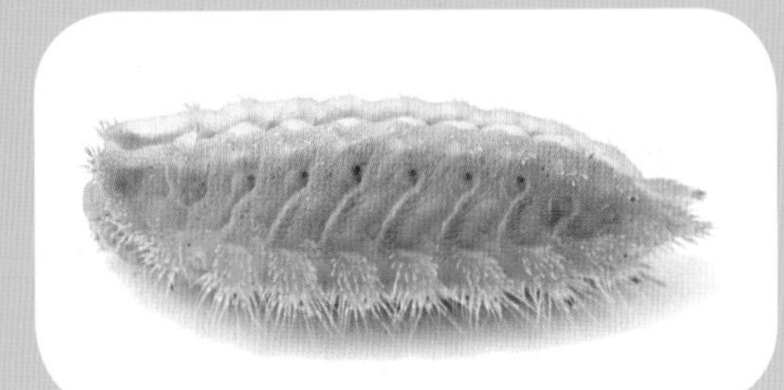

Hissssss!

Slithering down the branch, this green guy may look like a snake. And that's just the way he likes it. But the spicebush swallowtail is really a peaceful caterpillar that relies on mimicry to scare away predators. It even has a smelly "forked tongue" like a snake.

Instead of looking smooth and sleek like a snake, some caterpillars rely on horns to look as tough as possible.

Scientific Name: Papilio troilus
Size: 1.5 to 2 inches
Habitat: North America
Diet: Spicebush and other trees

Look Away!

Caterpillars aren't the only ones who think the more eyes the better. Many butterflies, reptiles, birds, and fish use eye spots to look big and bold.

Any Way You Slice It

A ferocious close-up highlights the shape of the mango tree borer. It may look like an alien, but its body resembles many other creatures on this planet. Insects are bilaterally symmetrical, which means the left side mirrors the right side. Like birds, fish, and mammals, they have mouths, ears, eyes, and noses on their heads. In contrast, snowflakes, cookies, and jellyfish display radial symmetry. They can be divided into wedges, and all the pieces will look the same. These animals tend to have mouths in the center of their bodies so they can slurp up a meal—wherever it comes from.

Scientific Name: Batocera rufomaculata
Size: 1.3 to 2.7 inches
Habitat: Caribbean, Africa, Middle East, Southeast Asia
Diet: Fruit trees

The word "insect" comes from a Latin word that was once used to describe small animals with bodies that appear cut or divided.

Tree Trouble

This beetle tunnels through the branches of mango trees and lays its eggs in the cracks of the trunk.

Sensory Overload

The head of a mosquito is highly sensitive. Massive eyes help mosquitoes find their next meal. Their antennae sense the speed of other mosquitoes' wings as they fly by. Mosquitoes also rely on scent, heat, moisture, and chemicals in the air to find each other.

Scientific Name: Culicidae
Size: .1 to .75 inch
Habitat: Wherever there is fresh water
Diet: Flower nectar and blood

Mosquitoes use tiny scales on their legs to trap air so they can float on water.

Ouch!

All mosquitoes have a nasty reputation for biting and spreading disease, but it's really just the females that are dangerous. They use the protein in blood to make eggs. Some target humans. Other species prefer bird blood or frog blood. Most aren't picky. They'll bite whatever animal they can find.

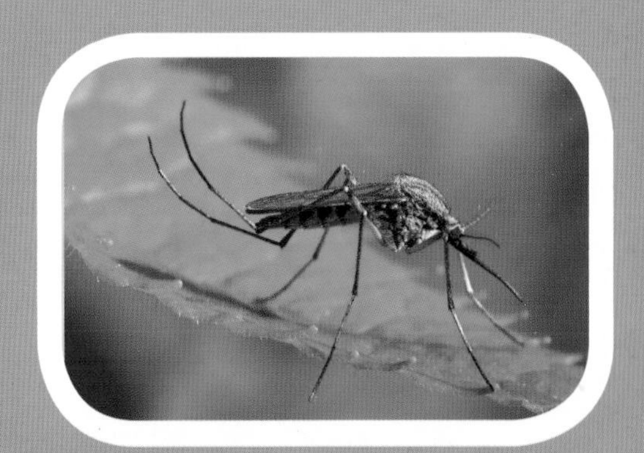

Smello to You!

Ants use their sense of smell to tell other ants hello, how to find food, and where to go. There are three types of ants: queens that lay the eggs, males that mate with the queen, and female workers that care for the queen and her young. Life inside the colony isn't easy, and ants aren't afraid to get bossy with each other. Their survival depends on it!

Scientific Name: Formicidae
Size: .08 to 1 inch
Habitat: Pretty much everywhere except the Arctic
Diet: Seeds, small insects, and nectar

The hair on a Saharan silver ant is used to deflect heat in extreme temperatures.

My, What a Big Head You Have!

Having extra large heads helps some ants attack other ants and tear apart prey. When big-headed ant colonies are under attack, they produce more soldiers that can fight back in a big way!

Spiraling Down
Down...
Down...
Down...

Do dark stairways ever lead anywhere good?
Depends what you're hungry for.

Slurp!

If you're an insect, chances are you're hungry for sugar! Some butterflies and moths don't have mouths at all. They do all the eating they will ever do as caterpillars. But those that have mouths usually have a proboscis. It works just like one of those crazy twisty straws you get at the circus. Butterflies and moths unfurl their long tongues to reach the sweet, sweet nectar inside flowers. When they're not sucking up sugar, the proboscis is coiled up inside their mouths.

Moths are nocturnal. More than 150,000 species hit the sky each night.

Scientific Name: Apatura iris
Size: Wingspan can reach up to 3.5 inches
Habitat: Woodlands of Central Europe and Asia

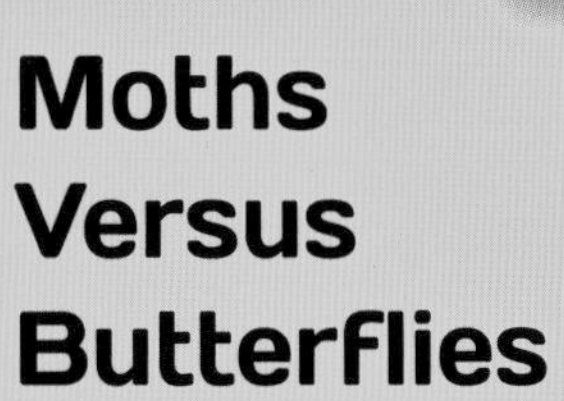

Moths Versus Butterflies

How can you tell the difference between moths and butterflies?

Moths		Butterflies
Feathery or ragged	**Antennae**	Long and club shaped
Hold their wings like a tent over their abdomen	**Wings**	Fold their wings over their backs
Smaller	**Size**	Larger
Often dull and brown	**Color**	Come in a rainbow of colors
Most are nocturnal	**Active**	Fly most often during the day
Builds a silk cocoon	**Metamorphosis**	Makes a hard, smooth chrysalis

Meet Mr. Weevil

Its long, black snout may look like an elephant's trunk, but the weevil is 1,500 times smaller than an elephant. Its long nose acts as a mouth and helps it dig holes. Different types of weevils have different snout shapes, depending on the shape of their favorite foods. These fellows are picky eaters. Most prefer to eat just one type of food. Give this bug a top hat and a cane, and it might become a proper gentleman.

Evil Weevils

These tiny creatures are famous for creating big trouble, and farmers loathe them. Each year millions of dollars of crops are destroyed by weevil activity.

Scientific Name: Sitophilus zeamais
Size: roughly .1 inch
Habitat: Tropical areas around the world
Diet: Wheat, corn, rice, and other grains

Weevils are also **known** as **"snout beetles."**

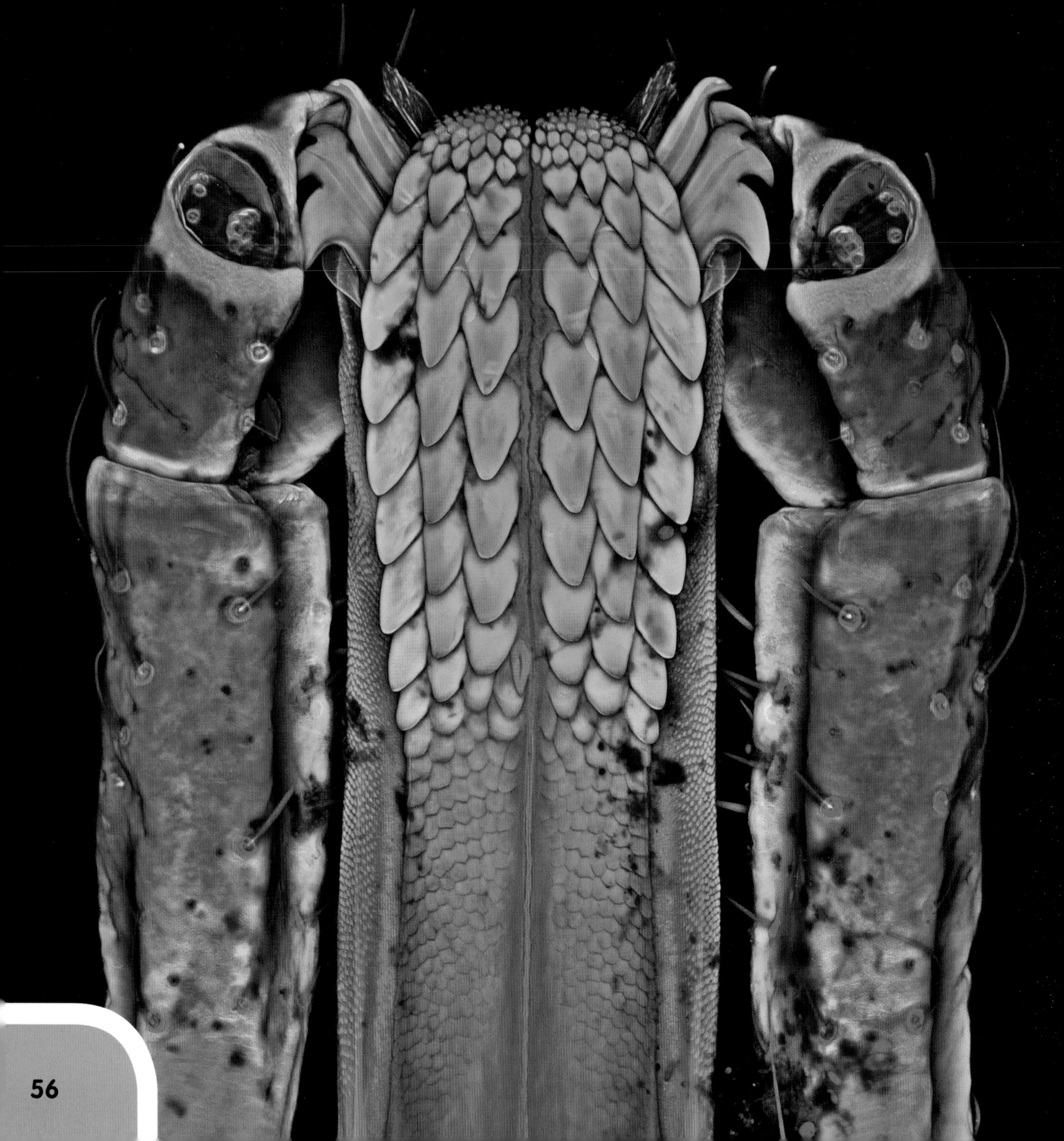

Ticked Off

That's a lone star tick giving you a long, hard look. These tough guys are famous for spreading disease. A single bite can even make some people allergic to meat!

Surviving the Spotlight

The rainbow colors in this image are the effect of micrography. Scientists use scanning electron microscopes (SEMs) to get way up close to their subjects. The work is done inside a vacuum to keep the process clean. Subjects are often stained or dipped in metal. To create an image, the SEM hits the subject with electrons and records how they bounce back.

Scientific Name: Amblyomma americanum
Size: .1 to .25 inch
Habitat: Meadows, woodlands, and forests in North America
Diet: Blood

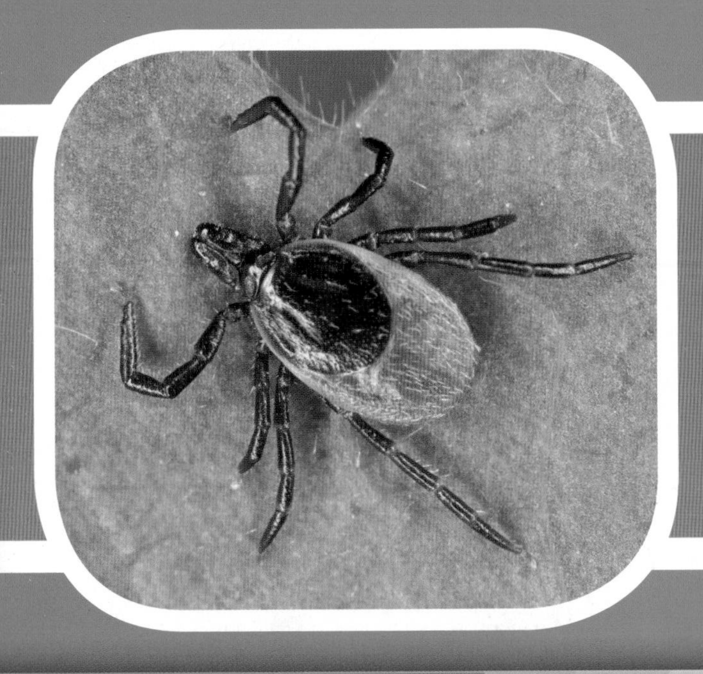

Micrography is a tough process, and most creatures don't make it out alive. But ticks are the first animals to ever be scanned with SEM and survive!

Bug or Beatle?

Can a bug be a beetle? Sure! But is a beetle always a bug? Not so fast. Many people use the word "bug" to refer to all different kinds of insects. But scientists use this word to refer to insects with a needle-like mouth, thick wings, and antennae with four or five segments. Jewel bugs like this colorful fellow may look like beetles, but are actually true bugs!

Project Noah

What can you do if you're backpacking across Mt. Kilamanjaro—or just in your own backyard—and you find a strange looking bug? Take a photo! Then log on to ProjectNoah.com to record and identify your find. Experts and amateurs use the site to track everything from jewel bugs to tigers.

Scientific Name: Scutelleridae
Size: .2 to .8 inch
Habitat: Parts of North America, central America, and Europe
Diet: Plants dissolved with saliva

Just like real jewels, jewel bugs come in a variety of colors.

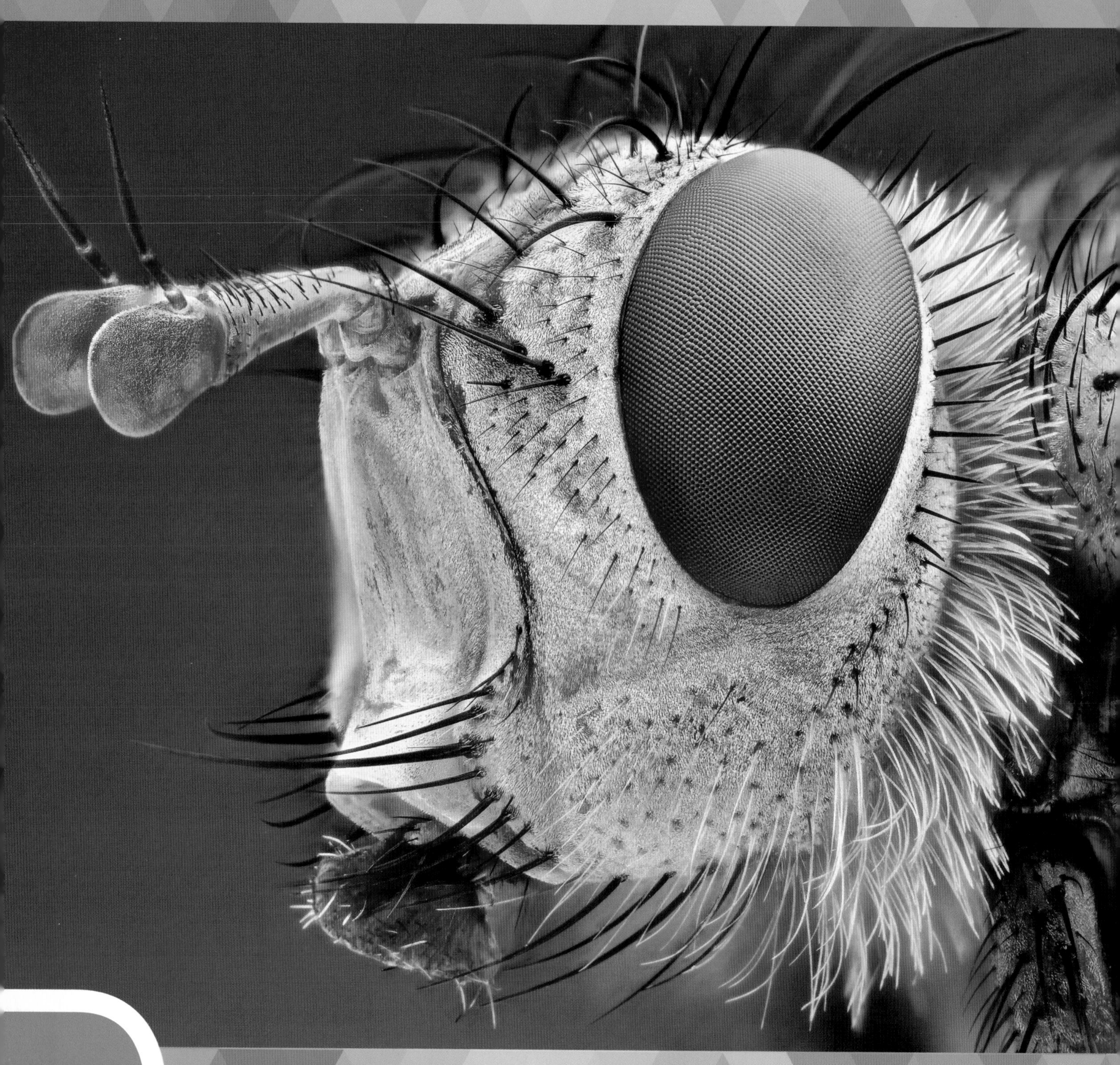

Save Don't Swat!

The hated housefly lives alongside humans around the world, gorging on garbage and spreading disease. It's a dirty job, but someone's got to do it. Like many insects, flies are decomposers. They eat rotting food, but they also help move the nutrients in that food back into the soil, where we can all use it.

Scientific Name:
Musca domestica
Size: .15 to .3 inch
Habitat: Spans the globe
Diet: Feces, sugar, blood, rotting food

A female housefly can lay more than 1,000 eggs in her lifetime!

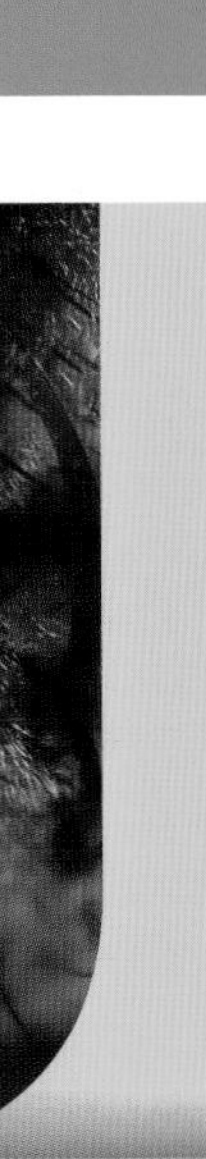

Highly Sensitive Hairs

Houseflies use hairs on their feet to taste food. Other hairs help flies sense air flow so they can steer clear of trouble when they're flying.

Behind the Lens

Now it's your turn! Grab a camera and start shooting whenever you see something that amazes you or makes you curious to learn more. If you want to go macro without spending too much money, snap a macro lens band over a cellphone camera. Whatever camera you use, these tips will help you get started.

The flash lights the subject.

The shutter acts like a camera, opening and closing to let light into the camera for short periods of time.

The lens is the curved piece of glass that light travels through before reaching a sensor or film inside the camera.

A tripod keeps the camera steady.

The size of the opening in the lens is the aperture. It's measured in fractions.

The focal point is the part of the image that's sharp.

The depth of field is the distance between the parts of an object that are in focus. In micro and macro photography, this distance is very small.

Some lenses have a short focal length and produce a wider angle of view. Other lenses have a longer focal length.

Aperture Scale

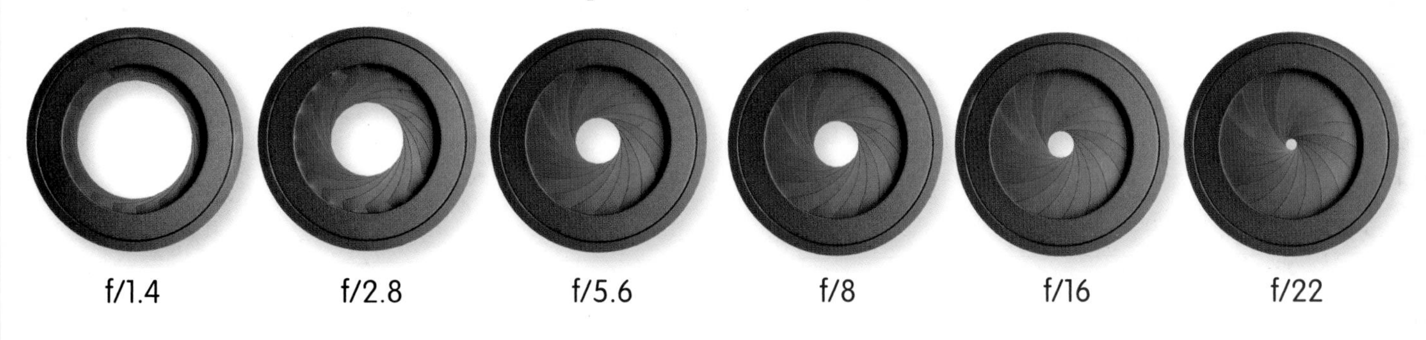

Index